Francis Poulenc

Sonata

for clarinet and piano

Revised edition, 2006

Edited by Millan Sachania

Clarinet part

Chester Music

à la mémoire d'Arthur Honegger

SONATA

for Clarinet in B♭ and Piano

FRANCIS POULENC

I

Allegro tristamente

très léger
molto

57
7
61
65
8 Très calme ♩ = 54
70
76
9 surtout sans presser
80
83
10
molto
pp doucement monotone
87
91
tr

96
mf
100
tr
[mf]
[p]
mf
p
11 Tempo allegretto ♩ = 136
105
p
[f]
110
115
p
12
p monotone
5
119
p
pp
123
126
8
pp
130
pp

II

Romanza

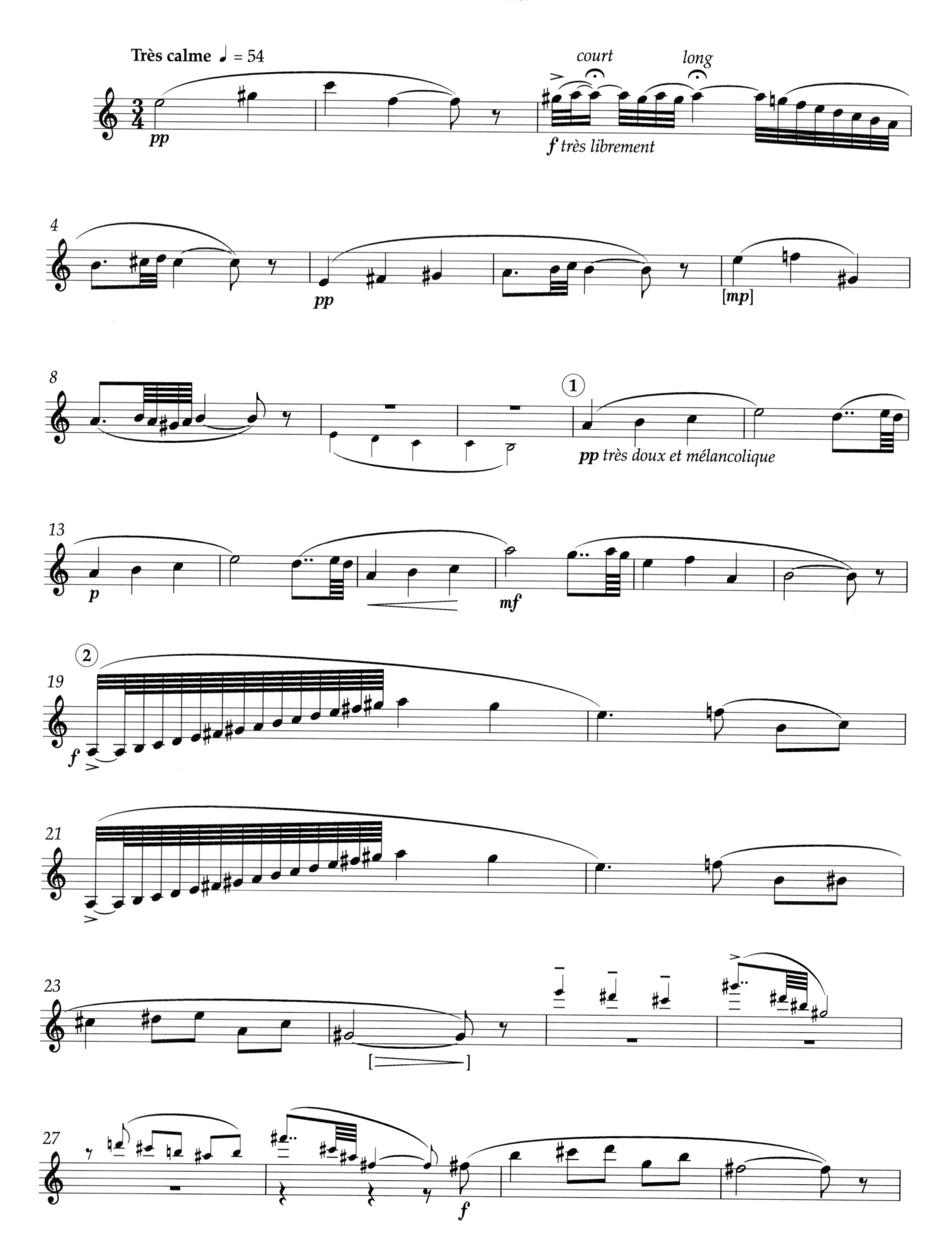
Très calme ♩ = 54
court
long
pp
f très librement
pp
[mp]
pp très doux et mélancolique
p
mf
f
f

3
31
mf
36
p
mf
4
42
mf
47
5
pp
52
f
57
p
6
mf
tr
63
pp
pp
68
ppp
7
mf
molto
73
pp
mf

III
Allegro con fuoco

25
4
28
31
34
5
39
42
céder un peu
6 a tempo subito
47
7
tr
53
(tr)

8
9
10
11
59
66
72
76
80
83
86
90
f
mf
ff
[>]

tr
12
13
14
Eté, 1962

Selected works by

Francis Poulenc

1899–1963

Piano Solo

Album of Six Pieces
- Mouvements perpétuels No. 1
- Presto from Suite in C
- Impromptu No. 3
- Française
- Novelette No. 1
- Promenade No. 1 (A Pied)

Five Impromptus

Mouvements perpétuels

Three Novelettes
- No. 1 in C major
- No. 2 in B♭ minor
- No. 3 in E minor (on a theme of Manuel de Falla)

Ten Promenades

Suite in C

Piano Duet

Sonata (Prelude–Rustique–Final)
- (also suitable for two pianos, four hands)

Chamber Music

Elégie for horn and piano

Mouvements perpétuels
- orchestrated by the composer for 9 players (1946)
- arr. Heifetz, violin and piano
- arr. Levering, flute and guitar
- arr. Levering, 2 guitars

Sextet for piano, flute, oboe, clarinet, horn and bassoon

Sonata for flute and piano

Sonata for oboe and piano

Sonata for clarinet and piano

Sonata for two clarinets

Sonata for clarinet and bassoon

Sonata for horn, trumpet and trombone
- (also transcribed Nestor for flute and guitar)

Trio for oboe, bassoon and piano

Rapsodie nègre for low voice and two violins, viola, cello, flute, clarinet in B♭ and piano

EXCLUSIVELY DISTRIBUTED BY

CHESTER MUSIC

(a division of Music Sales Ltd)
14/15 Berners Street, LONDON W1T 3LJ
Exclusive Distributors: Hal Leonard Europe Limited
Distribution Centre Newmarket Road,
Bury St Edmunds, Suffolk IP33 3YB

www.chesternovello.com

Order No. CH70972